REBELLION

by

George Forbes

REBELLION

Bonnie Prince Charlie and the 1745
Jacobite Uprising

by

George Forbes

© Published by Lang Syne Publishers Ltd., Clydeway Centre,
45 Finnieston Street, Glasgow G3 8JU.

© Published by Lang Syne Publishers Ltd, Clydeway Centre,
45 Finnieston Street, Glasgow G3 8JU.
Origination by Newtext Composition Ltd,
465 Paisley Road, Kinning Park, Glasgow G5 8RJ.
Printed by Dave Barr Print, Clydeway Centre,
45 Finnieston Street, Glasgow G3 8JU.

Contents

Prologue

ANY account of the 1745 Jacobite Rebellion must begin with an understanding of Charles Edward Stuart, 'Bonnie Prince Charlie' or 'The Young Pretender' as he was also known, because the events of that uprising make no sense without an appreciation of his personality. It all began and ended with him.

He was brave, dashing, handsome, audacious, energetic, full of fire and enthusiasm and in a sense the whole rebellion was symbolic of a personal revolt on his part against his dour, fatalistic, stoical father who had repeatedly failed in his attempts to regain the Crown for his dynasty.

The House of Stewart throughout history had seemed dogged by a cruel Fate. Their first four King Jameses had died by murder or misadventure, Mary, Queen of Scots, and Charles 1 had both been executed and other monarchs had suffered spells of exile. This bad luck had extended to Charles' grandfather, a staunch Catholic who had been usurped by the Protestant William of Orange and had sought sanctuary in France.

Charles' father, 'The Old Pretender', so mishandled the 1715 Jacobite uprising that he arrived in Scotland once his disorganised followers had been defeated and had to ignominiously return to the Continent.

Charles was brought up at various splendid courts in Italy and France where intrigue, expectation and frustration were constantly in the air. He breathed in this atmosphere of high ambition among the exiled Scottish aristocracy who had pinned their hopes on the House of Stewart and was constantly disappointed by his father's pessimism and caution.

Born in Rome in 1720, the Prince was a young man of spirit by 1745, bursting with plans and hopes for his lost kingdom.

He had that indefinable quality called charisma, a force of personality which could win the unconvinced to his side. Time and again, hardened, practical chieftains, who entered his presence determined to talk him out of this foolishness, left spellbound by his inspiring qualities to fight for his cause. This powerful aura, impossible to recapture over the centuries, is important to keep in mind as the drama unfolds and the events caused by his overwhelming presence run their course for, in theatrical terms, he was a star if ever there was one.

There was also a streak of the adventurer and gambler in his nature but he had some solid ground on which to base his dreams. England was at war with France and the Highlands had been stripped of good quality troops.

In addition, the unpopular Hanoverian King George 11 was viewed as distant and uncaring in London when it came to his Scottish subjects.

The Highlanders in particular were worried that the Industrial Revolution and English colonisation would destroy their way of life.

As usual, the Old Pretender was slow and unwilling to embark on anything rash and the French King also dithered over supplying invasion troops.

Resolving to go alone (apart from seven staunch supporters who became known as 'the Seven Men of Moidart'), Charles secretly sailed from France in July, 1745. It was now or never.

He left a note for his father which stated, "I will go if I have only a single footman - to conquer or die."

CHAPTER 1

The Landing

DISGUISED as a student priest, the Prince landed on the silver beach at Eriskay on August 3rd, 1745.

His first night on Scottish soil was a wet and windy one, a stark contrast to the pampered courts of Europe. The bedraggled party lodged in a decrepit croft and ate flounder over a peat fire.

The news right away was bad. The Macleods and MacDonalds of Skye were refusing to "come out" for the Stewart cause since the Prince had failed to bring French troops along on his 'invasion'. The first bit of advice Charles got from local clan chiefs was - go home. Typically, he shrugged this setback off and sent couriers over to the mainland to take the Fiery Cross round the glens to raise the clans.

Charles brought all his personal magnetism to bear on Ranald MacDonald and, by the time he had finished haranguing him with grand visions, the young chieftain was vowing to die for his Prince and, what was more important, promising to bring his clansmen along with him.

The Prince sent his ships away home to France, convinced the die was now cast and indeed the clans of Glencoe and Keppoch soon joined his swelling ranks.

Donald Cameron, 'Young Lochiel', met the Prince at Borrodale determined to talk him out of a revolt but he too was spellbound by the Young Pretender's charm and the forcefulness of his arguments. Charles also managed to convince him that France was bound to send support once the revolt was properly launched.

The royal red silk standard was unfurled at Glenfinnan at the northern end of Loch Shiel and hundreds of Highlanders with broadswords, muskets and shields flocked down over the heather-clad hills, their cheers and pipe music echoing round the glen.

The Prince made a brief speech and a war council was called. A few days later the small army marched through the mountains to Glengarry coun-

Prince's arrival at Eriskay.

try, gathering new recruits all the time like three hundred Stewarts of Appin and two hundred MacGregors from Balquidder.

Meanwhile, the Government in London had put a price of £30,000 on the Prince's head and the task of defeating him was placed in the hands of Sir John Cope, a dithering general further handicapped by hostile natives in the Highlands who kept misdirecting his small army of redcoats.

While Cope was finding his way through mountain passes to Inverness, the Jacobite army descended on Inveraray then marched to Blair Castle in Atholl where, for the first time since his arrival, he spent a civilised couple of days being well fed under a solid roof with proper sleeping accomodation.

Raising the standard at Glenfinnan.

In high spirits he entered Perth with his ragtag band of followers (now several thousand strong) and proclaimed his father King James.

In a month he had done more for the Stewart cause than his father had done in a lifetime.

Charles from a contemporary engraving.

CHAPTER 2
First Blood

NEW recruits flocked to the Prince's standard at Perth. The most important was Lord George Murray, a 51-year-old Jacobite veteran who was appointed the army's principal general. He was shrewd and practical and the only man in the Prince's immediate entourage not likely to be won over by charm. Stiff, austere, aloof, he also had an element of caution in his character which helped rein in some of the Prince's more reckless schemes and yet Murray's acumen often lacked that bravado vital for a daring escapade like the rebellion.

As it progressed a dichotomy began to appear between Charles' daring aims and Murray's more pragmatic approach. Perhaps the old soldier reminded the Prince of the Old Pretender and brought out some of Charles' latent ill-feeling against authority.

But all agreed on the next target - Edinburgh.

Cope had now decided to sail his army down the north east coast to the Firth of Forth and head off the Jacobites from the capital.

The rebels promptly set off on the march to Dunblane and when they passed Stirling Castle they were fired on by the garrison of government troops but the Highlanders remained calm and never broke step despite cannon balls whistling around them.

Charles visited Linlithgow Palace then the army closed in on Edinburgh. The city fathers, fearing a bloodbath and wholesale destruction, wisely decided that resistance was useless and, despite the fact that redcoats still manned the castle, a deputation was sent to the Prince pleading for mercy and time to organise surrender.

Meanwhile, Cope was disembarking his army at Dunbar so the Highlanders poured through the open gates of Edinburgh and geared themselves for battle.

Charles entered in triumph, his blue bonnet at a jaunty angle with a white cockade in it. He sported a tartan coat, red velvet trousers and military

Edinburgh - next target for the rebels.

Charles visited Linlithgow Palace.

Women swooned at Holyrood as the prince held court.

boots and as he trotted along to review his troops under Arthur's Seat he had never looked more handsome and dashing. Tall with brown eyes and fair skin, he won over many hearts that day and seemed well aware of the propaganda value his heroic appearance had on the wavering populace.

He was mobbed by crowds at Holyrood House, women swooned and men cheered.

Days of riotous celebration followed and the Jacobites could hardly believe their good fortune.

Cope had moved his troops nearer to the city at Prestonpans. Charles moved his army out of Edinburgh to meet him and told his followers,

"Gentlemen, I have flung away the scabbard; with God's help I will make you a free and happy people."

The Highlanders threw their bonnets in the air, gave whoops of delight and set out for Musselburgh.

A local laird's son came to Lord George Murray at midnight on the eve of battle and said he knew of a narrow track over a morass which led to the enemy camp.

As the sun began mistily to rise, the Highlanders, screaming their war cries, fell on Cope's surprised, half asleep men, decimating them with their claymores.

An imaginative view of the Highland army's camp at Edinburgh. From a contemporary engraving.

The battle was over in ten minutes. Hundreds of Government troops lay dead and dying while those who could galloped off in full retreat.

The psychological effect of this battle was devastating.

Scotland now belonged to the Jacobites, although there were still enclaves of troops at the castles of Edinburgh, Stirling and Dumbarton.

But to all intents and purposes Charles' course of action had been a total success and the Government in London now knew they had a full-scale rebellion on their hands which would only be curbed by drastic action.

A contemporary picture showing the Highland Army's success at Prestonpans.

CHAPTER 3

South

CHARLES knew that winning Scotland was not enough. England had to be conquered too before the House of Stewart could be re-instated to its rightful inheritance.

So a Jacobite war council met every day to plan the march south while couriers were sent throughout Scotland and to France to drum up reinforcements.

Meanwhile, Charles, now for the first time earning the soubriquet 'Bonnie', indulged in social pleasures.

He held public dinners with chosen officers and encouraged the general public to come and view him. He rode out virtually every afternoon to review sections of his army then he would receive his female admirers at a busy supper before attending a ball or a musical soiree. He was a striking figure, much sought after by Edinburgh society, and although he could have his pick of women he remained distant as if there were grander things on his mind (as indeed there were).

He kept his Highlanders well disciplined and in his own person tried to generate an aura of regal authority allied to dependability and normality. Various proclamations were issued to re-assure the populace that he had their interests at heart.

But time was passing and Charles was getting restless, being always the keenest to press on southwards at the first opportunity.

Recruitment proved slower than expected (an ominous sign) but fresh supporters did come in from the north east, Dundee and Lowland areas. But the pro-Government Campbells were also busy massing troops in Argyll and word was expected daily of enemy English forces marching north in large numbers.

However, the news from France was encouraging. The Pope had decided to finance the Stewart cause on the understanding that their restoration would also result in the reinstatement of Catholicism as a national religion.

Netherbow Port, gateway to the capital which Charles now controlled.

But King Louis XV was still dithering about backing the Prince properly and was confused about conflicting reports concerning support for the Jacobite cause in Britain.

Nevertheless, he sent an envoy on a fact finding mission and his arrival in Edinburgh was proof of the seriousness of French interest.

The Palace of Holyrood, base for pleasure and business.

Privateers were also busy ferrying across guns and ammunition from the Continent to the rebel army.

Arguments now arose in earnest between the Prince and his commanders, particularly Murray, about strategy.

Charles, of course, wanted to invade England as soon as possible even although his makeshift army of around five thousand might have to face 30,000 regular troops.

Murray was all for consolidating in Scotland, using it as a base while awaiting help from abroad.

Even at this stage some chiefs wanted to retreat to the Highlands where they could set up a Jacobite mini-kingdom, leaving England to a French invasion. The Highlanders even dreamed of building up a trained army of 25,000 which would take part in a pincer attack south aided by foreign allies.

But such plans, not as far fetched as they seemed, required time and that was something Charles was convinced he did not have. He had been around plotting Jacobite aristocrats all his life and knew procrastination was a way of life with them. Determined at all costs to win over the initiative again as soon as possible, the Prince used all his charm and wits to win over his general staff to his way of thinking.

One argument he kept putting forward was the weight of Jacobite support

Carlisle Cross and the Old Guard House - town's surrender raised Highlander's spirits.

in the north of England. He claimed English rebels would flock to his standard as soon as he had crossed the border.
  A compromise was reached. England was to be invaded if for no other
reason than that the rebel army could not sit on the defensive and await
the combined units of General Wade, the Duke of Newcastle and the Duke
of Cumberland to lumber north and annihilate them. But the invasion
would not take the direct route to London. Instead it would involve a cir-
cuitous route down the north west corner thus keeping the enemy guess-

Charles leads the march south.

ing while giving the French time to arrive and the English Jacobites to organise themselves.

In November the rebels crossed into England, boosted by money and arms from Spain. There were five thousand infantry and 500 cavalry and numerous camp followers and luggage trains making up the Jacobite army.

Carlisle surrendered and this raised the spirits of the Highlanders.

Lancaster and Preston were reached a week later but support for the Jacobites proved disappointing, only a trickle of recruits coming in.

The army pressed on, aiming for Manchester. Many people by the roadside wished the Prince well but declined to join his ranks.

He entered Manchester triumphantly, in the same style as his conquest of Edinburgh, and again he won over many female hearts.

But of the many Lancashire Jacobites he was counting on there was scant evidence, only three hundred volunteers joining up and many of them being poverty stricken with little to lose.

An acrimonious council of war was held on St. Andrew's Day and although the possibility of retreat became ever more real it was eventually agreed that they would continue on to Derby in the hope that greater numbers would rally to their standard.

They had still not come up against any serious opposition in England for the government forces were unclear as to what exactly Charles' plan of action was and until that unravelled the Hanoverians were unwilling to commit themselves in the field.

On December 5th Derby was reached. It was as far south as the Jacobites were to go and a decision was made there which sealed their fate.

CHAPTER 4

Derby

THE drastic decision to retreat back to Scotland had been in the offing for weeks, ever since it was cruelly obvious there was no mass support for the Prince in England.

Often it seemed as though the dynamo driving the rebels south was Charles' willpower and nothing else. At Derby that force ran out of energy.

Murray, who had only grudgingly invaded in the first place, was adamant that, from a purely military point of view, retreat was the only option. In this he may have been correct but was that the only factor to be taken into consideration?

Only a hundred and thirty miles down the road, London was in a panic, the whole country on a knife edge. In a sense going back was almost as bad as a defeat in battle. The army would be intact - just - but its purpose would be broken, its morale brought low, its power to intimidate or inspire shattered. And the populace were fickle. They could switch to the Jacobite side if success seemed imminent.

Certainly King George was getting ready to decamp. The novelist Henry Fielding said the capital was in a state of alarm and uproar. There were real fears the Highlanders would come marching over Westminster Bridge, pipes skirling, any day.

The Jacobite army had no advance intelligence system to keep it informed of enemy activity yet Charles seemd to sense that just one more push southwards would be enough to topple the Hanoverian throne. He argued vehemently that the positive psychological effect on the public of such a last, final, successful effort would far outweigh any hazards.

But Murray and his growing band of supporters argued that only proper support from English Jacobites and the French could justify a march on London - and neither was forthcoming as yet.

He was also worried that at least two Hanoverian armies lay behind them

People in England were hostile to the Jacobites.

somewhere to the north east and a third would have to be faced at Finchley before London could be taken. Even a militia mustered from the city's million inhabitants might have to be defeated by the harassed Scots who were foreign invaders a long way from home with an overstretched, tenuous supply line and hostility on all sides.

In fact, Murray's pessimism was ill founded whereas Charles, in retrospect, can be seen to have had a shrewder, intuitive grasp of the tense situation.

The military problems were not as dire as those arguing for retreat maintained. Wade's army was at Wetherby, too far away to pose a threat, while the army blocking the Jacobites' way at Finchley was an ill-disciplined rabble which would have scattered at the first clash of arms. Cumberland was also a good distance off at Lichfield and could only have faced the Highlanders with at most 4,000 troops exhausted after forced marches.

The Highlanders were in high spirits at Derby, in sharp contrast to their leaders. They had the same feeling as Charles that their star was in the ascendant and now was the time for boldness.

Charles used all his charm to persuade his officers to march on. He told them the English Jacobites would rise en masse when the rebels entered London but Murray said bitterly their so-called southern supporters were only Jacobites in the tavern. They were all mouth and no action.

But, ironically, even as the rebels argued, another ally was ready to help for King Louis had finally decided to act and had ordered an invasion of England, despatching the duc de Richelieu to organise the embarkation of 15,000 crack troops from the Picardy ports by the end of the month.

Tragically, Charles, standing alone against his officers, did not have this information to hand in time.

He ranted at them, "You ruin, abandon and betray me if you do not march on."

They remained impassive, for the first time unmoved by the Prince's powerful personality.

So the decision was taken, with only the Prince in dissent. Retreat it was to be.

Charles shouted as they walked out, "In future I shall summon no more councils since I am accountable to nobody for my actions but to God and my father and therefore shall no longer either ask or accept advice."

To the end of his days the Prince remained convinced that defeat had been forced on him at Derby by the lack of nerve of the chieftains. He was certain that just a few more days would have gained him the British

Highlanders trudged home in despair.

Crown. It is an argument historians will tussle with till Doomsday.

The decision to retreat had several immediate effects.

Any English or French support that had been gathering momentum faded away. Now the rebels were truly on their own.

And the morale of the Highlanders collapsed. They could not understand why they were now being ordered to turn around and trek back to Scotland when they had caught the tang of victory, when their blood was up and they were ready to do or die.

Now they openly wept and cast down their guns. Discipline did not collapse but there was a decline with more pilfering and desertion and ugly incidents with jeering townspeople as they walked despondently back north, their heads down.

The effect on Charles was devastating. On the march south he had been buoyed up with optimism, jauntily riding at the head of his men. Now he rode, totally depressed, in the rear as if loàthe to leave England. Whereas before Derby he had been sober, energetic and needing little sleep, now he drank constantly, slept late and became gloomy and lethargic.

Something went out of Charles at Derby and since he was the driving force of the whole army it doomed the Rebellion as well. That something was hope.

CHAPTER 5

Retreat

OF COURSE the Jacobite retreat proved a great boost to the morale of the Hanoverian forces. They saw clearly for the first time that the rebels had no grand, concerted strategy. There was no cohesion between English and French supporters. It had all been a great gamble, after all. The decision at Derby had revealed the Jacobites' hand to be mainly bluff.

The Duke of Cumberland, now convinced he had only a makeshift Highland militia to deal with, in particular vowed to pursue and annihilate the rebels and their cause once and for all.

Because of the Prince's sullen, desultory attitude to military matters, the Jacobite retreat was not as fast as it should have been.

Charles had to be talked out of spending a few days in Manchester but insisted on staying some time at Preston. He was determined that there should not be the impression of a full-scale rout. He wanted to retire with dignity.

Cumberland almost caught up with the rebels before the Scottish border but was delayed attending to false reports of a French landing.

Charles foolishly insisted that a token garrison of Jacobites be left in Carlisle Castle and these three hundred and fifty brave men were either blasted by Cumberland's cannons or later executed. It was a useless sacrifice and sadly indicative of the Prince's increasingly callous and fatalistic view of his Highlanders. It was an omen and also brought back memories of his father's gloomy stoicism in defeat. Perhaps Charles rationalised his position by blaming his followers for the retreat and in the process began to lose interest in their welfare.

The rebels crossed the Esk back into Scotland on the Prince's twenty fifth birthday - December 20th - and split into two columns, Murray heading up through Moffat to Glasgow while Charles travelled to Dumfries then wheeled up to Douglas Castle and Hamilton.

Charles entered a hostile Glasgow, determined to replenish his supplies

Carlisle, and its Castle, scene of massacre.

and get fresh footwear for his men whose round-trip in England alone had involved marching five hundred miles. The Lowlanders, generally of the mercantile trade and loyal to the Crown, viewed the uncouth Highlanders with ill-concealed distaste.

Charles reviewed his troops on Glasgow Green but there was none of that euphoria that had greeted his arrival in Edinburgh only a few months previously.

He spent a week in the city and the outlook for him remained bleak. Edinburgh had been re-occupied by the Hanoverians and General Hawley had raised gibbets in the expectation of hanging the Highlanders. Lord Loudoun also held Inverness with an army of redcoats.

However, on the positive side a second Jacobite army had "come out" in Aberdeenshire. Lord Lovat, after much prevarication, now supported the Prince and new recruits had been raised at Perth and Dunblane. Also, eleven hundred Irish mercenaries under Lord John Drummond had landed at Montrose. And even at this late stage there was still the possibility of support from France.

But, because of Charles' petulant decision after Derby that there should be no more councils of war, these events were not properly analysed and discussed.

Various options now lay before Charles so he moved his army near to Stirling while he considered what to do next. He came down with a bad

Clansmen headed north and tried to re-establish authority.

Lord Lovat supported prince after much prevarication.

case of influenza and lay in a fever for a fortnight while, in freezing mid-winter weather, his men billeted themselves as best they could in villages and farms round about.

The Prince was nursed by Clementina Walkinshaw who became his mistress.

The Jacobites took the town of Stirling easily enough but the Hanoverian garrison in the castle held out and Hawley decided to send a relief column from Edinburgh. This linked up with a Campbell militia from Argyllshire and mustered at Linlithgow.

The Jacobites occupied a ridge of moorland south west of Falkirk. Both armies built up their strengths, Hawley and the Prince arrived on the scene in their respective camps and both forces now numbered around eight thousand men each.

A storm burst and hail drove into the faces of Hawley's men. Visibility

Jacobites capture Stirling.

was poor yet Hawley ordered a charge and seven hundred dragoons advanced on the Jacobite lines. They were decimated by musket fire and the clansmen then charged, waving their broadswords, into the Hanoverian infantry, hacking their way through them until the redcoats broke and fled.

Clansmen charged the redcoats.

As dusk fell it was obviously a victory for the rebels but not as decisive as it might have been with better co-ordinated tactics and clearer weather. Hawley, through his own incompetence, had been badly mauled but his army could still regroup.

The Jacobites entered Falkirk but they should have pressed on to re-take Edinburgh. The old pre-Derby Charles would have done so. The present one rode off to the arms of Clementina and a warming tot or two of whisky.

The pointless siege of Stirling Castle continued while the chieftains grumbled about the lack of leadership and with good reason.

Cumberland arrived at Edinburgh and once more defeatism spread among the ranks of the Jacobite army. A retreat to the Highlands was advocated as the most prudent policy.

The Duke of Cumberland - his arrival in Edinburgh spread defeatism.

Charles was typically furious at this proposal, especially since he viewed Falkirk as an important victory. He was all for taking on Cumberland now while the morale of the rebel army was comparatively high and he argued that retreat would lead to a flood of desertions which would be unstoppable.

But, as at Derby, he was outvoted by his officers and had to reluctantly accept their verdict.

"Have I lived to see this?" he exclaimed and, angry and frustrated, held his head in his hands.

His army moved north to meet its end.

CHAPTER 6
Culloden

THE retreat northwards was chaotic and confused. As the Prince had predicted, many clansmen simply took off of their own accord, tramping homewards over the heather, convinced the Stewart cause was lost and determined to salvage what they could from the reckless adventure.

Those who remained with the rebel army were naturally depressed at the prospect of yet another withdrawal and they even left their wounded and prisoners by the roadside as they fled and valuable artillery was also dumped. Stores of ammunition at St. Ninian's church were accidentally ignited and the resulting blast was heard for miles around. To all intents and purposes the Jacobites were already a defeated army without having yet fought their final calamitous battle.

They crossed the Forth at the Fords of Frew and Charles found a billet at Drummond Castle and there was a full review held at Crieff at which it was found there had been a thousand desertions.

Angry words were spoken at a war council and the bitterness between Murray and Charles resurfaced. Tempers were short and each blamed the other for what was rapidly turning into a fiasco.

It was eventually decided to head for Inverness through the Highlands although Charles had wanted to go there via the north-east coast where he was still hoping for a French landing.

The Prince moved on to Blair Castle where he tried to rest his frayed nerves.

The Jacobites were fortunate that the bitter winter weather ruled out any serious pursuit by the Hanoverian forces who struggled northwards through Dunblane, Crieff and Perth where a stop was made to stock up with provisions and plan a Spring campaign.

Inverness was still held for the Crown by Lord Loudoun who was delighted when an informer told him that Charles was being entertained by the beautiful 23-year-old Lady Mackintosh, the 'Colonel Anne' who had raised

Detail from a contemporary engraving 'An Exact View of the glorious victory ... at Culloden'. In the background are Inverness and the Moray Firth. From a woodcut of October, 1746.

her clan for the Prince against her husband's wishes, at Moy Hall.

Loudoun quickly assembled 1,500 troops, threw a cordon round the town to prevent any warning reaching Charles then marched out at night towards Moy.

Fortunately for the Prince, a 14-year-old innkeeper's daughter learned of

Detail from a contemporary engraving 'A Representation of the Battle on Drunmossie Moor near Culloden' (on horse-back in the left foreground are 'The Young Chevalier' and 'The Chevalier's Man Sulivan').

what was afoot from some officers she was serving and she ran barefoot to the home of Lady Mackintosh's mother who in turn sent off a boy to raise the alarm.

He successfully evaded the Government troops and reached Moy Hall in time to get the household out of their beds.

Charles escaped to the lochside in a nightgown while a local blacksmith

Government forces retreated in panic.

and four other men successfully bluffed the Hanoverians into thinking the whole Jacobite army was lying in wait for them in the dark. Shouting orders to non-existent regiments and firing volleys at Loudoun's troops, their subterfuge was so successful that the government forces panicked at the thought that they had been tricked and retreated pell-mell back to Inverness. This became known as the 'Rout of Moy' and proved a badly needed propaganda boost for the Jacobites.

Charles, shivering in nightgown and slippers, contracted pneumonia as a result of this incident and was out of action throughout February.

Thousands of rebels were gathered for an assault on Inverness but Loudoun compounded his humiliation at Moy by deciding to abandon the city and flee north via the Kessack ferry to the Black Isle.

In driving blizzards the Jacobite army now converged on Inverness where they were given badly needed warmth and shelter.

The Hanoverians, organising fresh relays of troops and supplies at Perth, eventually set off for Aberdeen through atrocious weather where they regrouped to plan their next move.

With Charles lying ill at Culloden House on the outskirts of Inverness, the clansmen, boosted by new recruits from Clan Grant, felt free to go out and do what they did best - harry the enemy with quick raids.

Fort Augustus was attacked, taken and pillaged in two days and Fort William was besieged.

Loudoun's forces were dispersed at Dornoch after Highlanders crossed the Moray Firth in fishing boats, successfully avoiding Royal Navy cruisers in a thick fog. This now meant the Jacobites had no enemy in their rear and could face Cumberland's forces with that re-assurance to bolster them.

Murray sallied south with his Atholl brigade, met up with Cluny MacPherson and his regiment in Badenoch and took thirty government posts or blockhouses simultaneously in the early hours of March 16th. Detachments of thirty Highlanders took each little stronghold without a casualty, bringing in hundreds of prisoners.

Murray went on to besiege Blair Castle, now occupied by the Hanoverians, but had to give up and retreat north when Charles refused to sanction sending him reinforcements.

Jacobite morale began to rise and there was even talk that they could carry on for years if necessary with this type of guerrilla warfare.

But there was always the looming threat of Cumberland which would have to be dealt with in a pitched battle at some stage.

Impatient for action, the obese, luxury loving but bloodthirsty Cumberland set off on the march in April, heading straight for the rebels, determined to snuff them out once and for all.

Ironically, the rise in Jacobite fortunes had happened while Charles was ill but now he arose from his sickbed to face a series of crises.

His army was cold, hungry and poorly paid. The latter situation was not helped when a Jacobite ship from France, laden with gold, ammunition and two hundred top-notch re-inforcements, was chased by Hanoverian cruisers in the Pentland Firth until she ran aground and was stormed by redcoats.

Charles decided to put on a show of optimism and gave a number of balls at which he danced all night with seeming delight, keeping his female partners in high spirits.

He did not have the resources to go out and meet Cumberland so had to wait until he approached closer.

But the Highland detachments were now widely dispersed over the surrounding countryside. Of a full army of around eight thousand, the Prince would only be able to muster five thousand.

Instead of indulging in dances, Charles would have been better employed planning in detail the defeat of Cumberland but by this stage fatalism seems to have become entrenched in his thinking, reminiscent of his father's gloomy, placid acceptance of whatever the future had to offer.

As Cumberland doggedly advanced from the east, there were ample

Jacobite ship was chased and ran aground in the Pentland Firth.

A contemporary print showing the Battle of Culloden.

opportunities to stop or at least harry his army in the glens and along the rivers which separated the Hanoverians from the Jacobites but no attempt was made to take advantage of the terrain to rain down attacks. This incompetence on the part of the rebels was to prove fatal.

Charles chose Drummossie Moor beside Culloden House as the scene of the climactic battle of his campaign and drew up his army there on April

15th. Murray and the clan chiefs objected to the site as unsuitable but Charles was convinced it was ideal. It was the last time his force of argument was to win the day and it was to have grim consequences.

Cumberland's troops had stopped at Nairn and the rebels decided a night raid on the sleeping army might prove successful. They had rousing memories of the dawn onslaught on Cope's redcoats to encourage them.

Charles wanted personally to take part in this audacious scheme and was in manic high spirits as they set out in the darkness.

But due to a thick fog and the rough terrain which included bogland and dykes and an unforeseen wall that blocked their route, the columns of men slipped behind schedule.

By 1 a.m., when they should have been slaughtering redcoats, the rebels were still four miles away, trying to find their way forward.

As stragglers tried to catch up with the van of the army gathering where a river had to be crossed, Murray realised the attack would have to be abandoned as dawn was rapidly approaching.

Charles, of course, was bitterly disappointed and felt his officers had let him down, just as at Derby and Falkirk.

So the men turned around and trudged wearily back to their lines on Drummossie Moor.

Cumberland's spies heard of this failure and the Hanoverians decided to take advantage of it by marching at once on the rebels.

Even at this late stage, Charles still had various options. He could have retired to Inverness and invite a siege which would have been costly and dangerous for the redcoats. The Jacobite army could have dispersed and reformed at a pre-arranged time and place later in the Spring. Or they could have fought on better chosen ground than that on which they now stood.

But the angry, frustrated, disillusioned Prince rejected impatiently all these options and, after the fiasco of the night march, was determined to face Cumberland's men and have it out once and for all.

Around five thousand tired, hungry, cold Jacobites now gathered to meet Cumberland's eight thousand seasoned, refreshed, disciplined redcoats.

Charles could have called on another 3,500 men if he had just waited another day for many were scattered foraging for food, manning outposts or simply lying exhausted and asleep in the heather.

But the petulant Prince was adamant there would be no further loss of face on his part. He was sick of the defeatism of his officers and was resolved to stand and fight, to do or die.

The Prince rode among his men, trying to encourage them. By 11 a.m. both armies faced each other across marshy terrain, two and a half miles apart.

Two hours later Cumberland's cannonade began. Salvoes of cannon balls cut swathes in the packed ranks of the Highlanders who simply had to stand and take it.

A Highlander equipped for battle.

By contrast, the Jacobite artillery was woefully inadequate. They had no professional gunners and the ordinance was antiquated and ineffective.

The Prince, who had difficulty seeing what was going on due to an ill chosen vantage point, eventually gave the belated order to charge but some of the exasperated Highlanders, determined to die in battle rather than on a shooting range, had already advanced with the cry "Claymore" so that the attack was badly co-ordinated.

A British dragoon in the Government cavalry force

In thick gunsmoke, the heroic rebels bore down on th
and cleaving their way through the ranks, and burst th
of the Hanoverian army in a welter of bloodshed and
   But the running Highlanders were mown down by w
unbroken ranks of the Hanoverians' second line, gr
- kneeling, stooping, standing, all with muskets coc
staggered on were stabbed by bayonets.

Redcoats move in.

The Jacobites had taken horrendous casualties in the carnage of a few brief minutes and tried to get back to their own ranks over the dead and dying bodies, four deep, of their comrades.

Further casualties were inflicted by flanking raids from the Campbells who were on the Government side, their claymores scything down fellow Highlanders.

Cumberland's cavalry advanced and met head-on a furious mounted charge from a hundred desperate rebels who saved their army from being surrounded. In savage fighting, the superior Government forces were forced to give way.

But by this time a third of the Jacobite army was out of action and casualties were mounting all the time.

The Prince tried to rally his dishevelled, disorganised men streaming back from the advancing enemy lines. He yelled at them, as his wig blew off, that he would dismount and personally lead them in a last charge. Many who heard him could only speak Gaelic and did not understand his gallant words.

He was eventually persuaded by his immediate entourage to leave the battlefield, looking back gloomily at his brave Highlanders.

He missed much of the butchery that now took place on the bloodsoaked moor. Cumberland ordered that no mercy be shown to the rebels and wounded men were given no quarter. Even sleeping clansmen who had taken no part in the battle were shot or bayoneted as they lay on the ground. The actual fighting had lasted less than an hour.

The Prince rode off towards the safety of Fraser country to assess the extent of the damage done to his cause.

It was colossal. In that brief spell on Drummossie Moor, despite the reckless bravery of their supporters, the banner of the House of Stewart had been lowered forever. Not even guerrilla tactics were feasible now.

Charles sent out messages to the effect that it was now every man for himself. Around four thousand Jacobites had rallied at Ruthven and when they were given the news they felt betrayed. Their laments rent the air. They knew what to expect from Cumberland and were desperate to carry on the fight.

The Hanoverians now introduced their own Final Solution to the Highland problem. Rebels were rounded up and summarily executed, farms and crofts were burned, cattle and property confiscated, women raped.

Cumberland was given the nickname 'Butcher' which has stuck with his memory ever since. Only six leaders of the rebellion were taken alive and five of them were executed. More than nine hundred rebels were transported as convict labour to America and the West Indies while others died in English jails or on prison hulks on the Thames.

The clans who had taken part in the rebellion were dispossessed and their land sold cheaply to rival neighbours. The clan systen was smashed and the whole way of life of the Gael was systematically destroyed as Hanoverian troops swarmed over the countryside throughout the summer of 1746, being given a free hand to destroy the 'savages' they came across.

The luckier Jacobites escaped abroad to a life of banishment, like Murray, but everyone who had supported Charles had their lives ruined as a result.

Farms and crofts were burned in an orgy of violence after the battle.

The Prince was forced to take to the heather, a price on his head.

Now that the responsibility of leading a rebel army was gone, Charles experienced an exhilirating sense of freedom, spiced with danger.

He now embarked on the most romantic five months of his colourful career.

CHAPTER 7

In the Heather

RESTING by day and travelling by night, the Prince and a few companions galloped through the Highlands, skirting lochs and plunging down glens in the moonlight, sleeping in friendly crofters' cottages.

A reward posted for him, the redcoats hot on his trail, Charles made his way westwards towards the islands where he hoped he might find a boat for France.

The horses were abandoned and long marches took the party over some of the wildest and most spectacularly beautiful countryside in Scotland.

Eventually, he reached the coast and set off at night by boat across the Sound of Arisaig, running into a gale which, fortunately for him, also drove them away from three English men o' war. Bailing hard, almost overcome with seasickness, the seven men on board managed eventually to land at Benbecula between North and South Uist although the storm was still blowing hard.

After resting in a cottage, the party set off for Stornoway but they were washed ashore at Scalpay.

After warm meals, drams of whisky and some sleep between clean sheets, all supplied by friendly islanders, they set off once more, this time on foot but got lost in boggy country where news was brought to the Prince that he was liable to get a hostile reception in Stornoway, the populace having been roused by a local minister.

Cold, tired, wet, the Prince and his small loyal band stayed cooped up in a derelict hut, watching the patrols of British ships now scouring the coastline.

They took to sea once more and were pursued by H.M.S. Furnace but evaded her by steering into shallows.

A grim cat-and-mouse game between the Prince's party in their little boat and the lumbering men o' war now ensued among the Hebridean islets but the Prince managed to give his pursuers the slip every time.

Glen where fugitives hid.

Charles was depressed but uncomplaining as the fugitives survived on trout, duck, eggs and biscuits while their spirits were fortified by wine, brandy and whisky, all supplied by local fishermen and crofters. Throughout all his time in the heather, no-one ever remotely considered betraying Charles for the £30,000 Government reward on his head, such was the bond of loyalty among the Highlanders, rich and poor alike.

The Prince hid out for three weeks on South Uist and his companions

Escape in wild weather.

noticed that severe mood swings seemed to effect him and these were compounded by his increasing intake of alcohol. As the news arriving from the
mainland became bleaker, he drank more and was able to stand his liquor
when even sturdy Highlanders lay comatose on the floor.

Troops landed near his hide-out and Charles had to flee once more, crossing and recrossing from island to island in wild weather to avoid government patrols scouring land and sea for him.

There were a few narrow escapes and often the beleaguered party had to
spend cold nights out in the open, plagued by midges, soaked with rain.

The net was now tightening and often redcoats were spotted in time less
than a mile away.

On the west coast of South Uist the Prince came across 23-year-old Flora
MacDonald, an admirer of his.

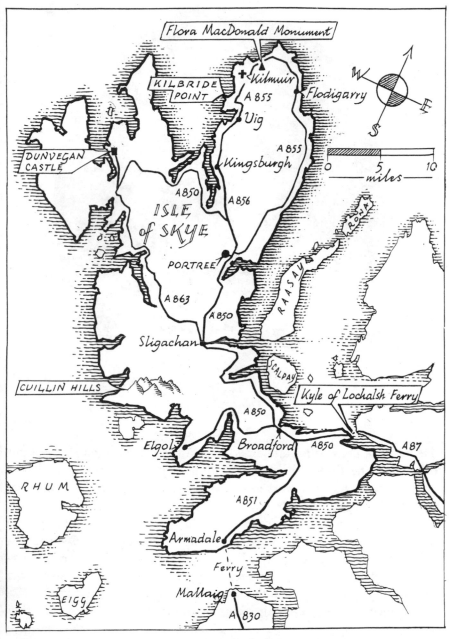

Isles where Charles hid.

Flora MacDonald

He stayed at her shieling and dined on a dish of cream and a plan was put to her that the Prince should dress up as her female servant and thus escape to Skye. Charles worked his famous charm on Flora and won her round to this daring scheme.

Sheltering in rocks and bothies to avoid the troops now all over the island, the Prince made his way to Rossinish where he met up with Flora and donned the disguise of 'Betty Burke', her servant. This involved wearing a petticoat, gown and mantle together with shoes, stockings and a wig and cap. They then set off across the Minch 'over the sea to Skye'.

The Prince sang to keep their spirits up in the darkness but yet another Hebridean gale arose, whipping the water into a fury. They managed to reach the Skye shoreline safely where sentries ordered them ashore. The party rowed off, shots were fired but they made good their escape round a headland and landed near the house of a Jacobite supporter.

Bonnie Prince Charlie and Flora meet for the first time at Ormaclett on the Isle of South Uist, June 20, 1746.

They then set off to walk inland but encountered a congregation return-ing from Sunday service who seemed curious about the odd appearance of 'Betty Burke'.

Eventually, the party reached the safety of a rebel's house where they had a good supper and lots to drink. They toasted their success in avoiding capture.

Flora received a lock of the Prince's hair as a keepsake and he promised he would shower her with riches once he was restored to his kingdom.

Charles, now changed into Highland dress, set out for Portree and crossed to Raasay Island which had been decimated by Cumberland's troops. Three hundred cottages had been burned to the ground and the fields laid waste.

But the islands were becoming too hot for him so he crossed back over to the mainland, landing at Mallaig.

The hunt for him now intensified, passes were blocked, patrols covered the countryside night and day and reinforcements poured in from England. Anyone suspected of helping him was arrested and interrogated.

But his secret network of Jacobite sympathisers kept Charles beyond the reach of Government forces and the reward (a million pounds by today's

Charles as Betty Burke.

Flora and Charles dodged the pursuers.

Engraving depicting when the French Commanding Officer surrendered Carlisle to the Duke of Cumberland.

standards and undreamed-of wealth to a poor crofter) proved a useless enticement to the loyal Highlanders.

The brutality of the Hanoverians after Culloden also stopped any Highlander from helping them.

Darting in and out of inlets, sleeping rough, the Prince and his small band evaded the redcoats' lines of forts and cordons.

Pressing northwards, they slipped past Hanoverian camps in the dark and the Prince learned French scouts from ships offshore were busy looking for him.

'John of Gant in Love, or Mars on his knees'
A caricature published in 1749, during Cumberland's unpopularity after the rebellion.

'The Old Scourge return'd to Barrels'
Colonel Rich maintaines discipline in his regiment after their return from Culloden.
From a contemporary satirical print.

Drawing showing the advance into England. The Highland army arrives at Manchester.

Duke of Cumberland and troops in pursuit of Jacobites.

Charles sheltered in Cluny MacPherson's 'Cage', a cave chiselled into the face of Ben Alder, hidden by bushes, converted into a makeshift home.

He received word there were two French ships anchored in a sea loch to the west. He successfully embarked and arrived on the Continent where he was hailed as a hero.

Certainly during his time on the run the Prince had shown great tenacity and endurance. Apart from the ordeals of cold, hunger and exhaustion, there was the ever present threat of violent death. Charles was convinced (possibly with good reason) that he would be assassinated by his enemies before they would ever allow a possibly embarrassing trial to go ahead that might turn him into a martyr.

This period of his life, with its narrow escapes, midnight forays, moonlit sails, storms, pursuits and flights, enhanced the 'Bonnie Prince Charlie' legend and gave his personality a new glamour it had lost after the debacle of Culloden.

This period of his life, with its narrow escapes ... enhanced the "Bonnie Prince Charlie" legend.

CHAPTER 8

'Will Ye No' Come Back Again?'

FOR Charles, as indeed for the whole Jacobite cause since he was its personification, it was now downhill all the way. But for a while this was not obvious.

He was feted as a hero throughout the courts of Europe as tales of his adventures spread and women especially flocked to see him.

He was guest of honour at countless banquets and balls and this frenetic social activity initially helped subdue his misgivings about the future. For that did not appear quite as golden as the present adulation might suggest.

While his followers in Britain were rounded up, jailed or hung, the French began to cool towards the Jacobite cause which received a further blow when Charles' brother Henry was made a Cardinal by the Pope. The Prince realised this had reduced his chances of seizing the throne in the Protestant United Kingdom even more. He was furious and his temper was not improved when King Louis ordered him out of France following a peace treaty with Britain. Charles refused to go and had to be unceremoniously seized by the military authorities and escorted out of the country. It was a grave embarrassment to the Stewart cause and one which could not have suited the Hanoverians better.

The Old Pretender still maintained a court at a Roman Palazzo where he sank into senility while his once dashing son descended into drunken debauchery.

Charles embarked on a series of disasterous love affairs, each more sordid than the one before as polite society began to shun him. He moved restlessly through various aristocratic circles in Europe, still dreaming in his cups of a glorious restoration.

He took to donning disguises and travelling under assumed names, plotting fresh phantom rebellions. He even sailed secretly to London in 1750

... they had a daughter ... on whom Charles doted ...

after mistakenly being informed that King George was on the point of death. After a fortnight in hiding, during which he went through the motions of giving up Catholicism for Anglicanism to please his English Jacobite supporters, he skulked back to the Continent.

For three years he plotted to have King George assassinated but his hare-brained schemes were exposed by English spies and nothing came of them.

Clementina Walkinshaw returned to become his mistress once more and they had a daughter, Charlotte, on whom Charles doted.

Obese, dissipated, bitter and violently argumentative, Charles now no longer cut the dashing figure he once had.

His mood swings became more erratic and after eight years Clementina left him, taking her daughter with her.

Following his father's death, Charles lived in Rome as Baron Renfrew and by the age of fifty had become swollen legged, lethargic, bloated, red-faced and deeply melancholic.

Perhaps realising he needed a positive jolt in his life, he married Louise of

Stolberg, an 18-year-old, charming princess, in 1772.

He gave up drinking for a while and found a new zest but this was short-lived and soon his new bride tired of him. She fell in love with a poet and Charles, who had failed in the bedroom, took to beating her. She fled to a convent and Charles then took to six bottles of wine a day.

His physical condition deteriorated and he suffered from sores, piles and delirium tremens. His daughter returned to nurse him and he died in her arms in Rome in 1788. At the time of his death he was calling himself the Count of Albany.

Canova designed a Stewart monument in the Chapel of the Virgin in St. Peter's. Under busts of the Old Pretender and his son halfway up a pillar are the words 'The Last of the Royal House of Stewart'.

The great adventure was over.

CHAPTER 9

Aftermath

BONNIE Prince Charlie was gone but he was certainly not forgotten.

A treasury of Jacobite songs extolled the romantic excitement of his Scottish revolt while novelists like Scott and Stevenson spun wild tales around his exploits, melodramatic enough in themselves in real life.

To the lucrative tourist trade, which he was not to foresee, he bestowed countless millions of pounds in revenue and his name has become attached to numerous commercial products.

But even to this day, despite the glamorous allure of his name, Charles Edward Stuart remains a deeply ambivalent figure in the Scottish psyche.

The destruction of the Highland way of life which he brought about would have happened anyway but it need not have been so bloody or so harrowing.

And it must be remembered that the Scots themselves had a hand in his downfall. After all, many of Cumberland's troops were Lowlanders and many of the clans stayed loyal to the Crown. Levies such as those made up from the Campbells eagerly assisted the Hanoverian forces and settled old scores in the process. It wasn't just the English who let Charles down. His cool reception in Glasgow was symptomatic of how much of Scotland - increasingly mercantile, industrial, Protestant and U.K. oriented - viewed his disruptive incursion. And his Highlanders, traditional predators on the richer farmlands in the south, were viewed with hostility in many of the settled, more civilised towns they marched through.

But despite all that, there was something dashing and daring about the 1745 rebellion which caught the public imagination. Perhaps Scott encompassed the dichotomy best when he said his heart was with it but his head warned 'no'.

The whole enterprise basically revolved around the decision taken at

Derby and in this Charles, in retrospect, might be seen to have had the better, intuitive grasp of the situation.

Having come so far it seemed folly to turn back. Yet in such a course it is the sudden, dramatic gesture that often wins the day and in a sense Charles had a right to feel betrayed.

Certainly his Highland troops, like most Scots soldiers before and since, much preferred being on the offensive and their spirits sank as they had to scurry back north.

The trouble with the Jacobites was that they lacked a military genius of the calibre of Montrose or Bruce. Murray and the like were competent at best but often too conservative in their thinking and too pessimistic. Charles was surely correct with his emphasis on dash and bravado to carry the day.

But these qualities in the Prince brought their own problems.

It was his own impetuosity that started the '45 Rebellion in the first place and he always had to be dashing a few paces ahead of events and certainly ahead of the thinking of his officers. The pace had to be fast and furious, difficult for any mere mortal to sustain indefinitely.

He was out on a limb from the word go and knew it but he had the courage of his convictions and a recklessness that just might have succeeded if allowed full rein.

At Derby he said help would come from France. He was right, it had already been set in motion but there simply had not been enough time to inform the rebels.

He said English Jacobites would flock to his banner. He may just have been right there, as well, for lack of communication and co-ordination had left many of them out of touch or lukewarm to the confused information concerning rebel movements. Again there was not enough time for the various sympathetic elements in the country to coalesce around the Prince's retinue.

But time was always against him. He had to be one step ahead of everybody. He had to bluff his supporters into continuous support and he had to hoodwink his enemies. Considering he had only his natural abilities to work with, certainly at first, the Prince achieved much in a brief, hectic spell.

Even after Derby there was nothing inevitable about defeat. He could still call on considerable numbers of fresh recruits. He could still inflict damage on the enemy (witness Falkirk). And, as was seen prior to Culloden, the Highlanders made some brilliant forays into their enemies' ranks and performed successful commando raids, exploits at which they were expert.

Properly handled and with expert generalship, the Jacobite army could have proved very difficult to defeat in the Highlanders' native mountain fastnesses and this would have given Charles' allies the much needed time to send help from abroad.

But one of the weakest elements of the whole rebellion was also, ironically, its strongest point - Charles himself.

When he was in a good mood with events going his way, the revolt rolled along successfully, gaining its own momentum. When he was depressed over a setback, the whole enterprise seemed to go into reverse gear.

The Rebellion depended far too much on the vagaries in mood of the Prince and he often displayed manic depressive tendencies.

Prior to Derby he had been in high spirits then he fell into a black despair, understandable given the circumstances but also highly dangerous in the rebels' precarious, exposed position.

After Falkirk he had been elated then was cast down as his officers voted to retreat.

Finally, on the night march to Nairn he had been full of fight but then, as it all went wrong, he once more went into a black mood - but this time with almost suicidal consequences on Drummossie Moor. It was almost as if he willed his cause and army to destruction and would certainly have ridden to his death if he had not been restrained by those around him.

Seldom can a battle have been so mishandled, from the choosing of the ground to the deployment of the rebel ranks. It showed the Prince at his bad tempered worst and he must shoulder the blame for the massacre that ensued.

His ill health, which included influenza and pneumonia in the months between Derby and Culloden, could have been a contributory factor in his rash decisions as indeed his heavy drinking as well which began after the retreat northwards. It was all symptomatic of a deeper malaise, an inherited trait from his father which succumbed to adversity with an ingrained sense of doom. Perhaps there was a curse over the House of Stewart but, if so, it was more likely to be in the melancholic mentality of the family members than anything supernatural.

Charles always maintained in later life that he never believed that his adventure would wreak such havoc on his supporters and when he was first told of Cumberland's vengeance he dismissed the horror stories as wild exaggerations. When he realised they were true, he was shattered with

A soldier of the Black Watch in 1760.

A piper of the 93rd Highlanders in the Rob Roy tartan in 1845.

guilt and could often be heard yelling the one word "Scotland" during his many later nightmares.

His alcoholism was a reaction to the responsibility he felt for the destruction he had left in his path and it is true that he would never have embarked on his rash adventure if he had thought the results might prove so calamitous to so many.

It is difficult to sympathise with the Prince in his ageing, drunken loneliness when one thinks of all the men, women and children killed or maimed or ruined in some way through his incompetence, egotism and selfish emotionalism.

A childish self-pity ran through Charles' character, along with self-seeking and self-loathing, and probably the seeds of destruction were there in him from the beginning.

But at the end of the day what a tale he left behind, what a romance his life was, what a meteor he is in British history, what an inspiration he will remain to future romantics and artists just as he always has been since he stepped ashore that wild summer night all those years ago.

The "Feile" - or "Great Kilt" as worn in ancient times

"Red Coat" Government infantryman of the mid-eighteenth century.

Many Scots are still proud of the Jacobites' achievements against all odds. They dream of what might have been and view the final defeat as an epic tragedy like the last verse of an old Gaelic ballad.

The most poignant of all the fine Jacobite songs is 'Will Ye No' Come Back Again'. In one sense Charles Edward Stuart has never really left the hearts of many Scots. And never will.

For he is the embodiment of Scotland - courageous, spectacular, colourful, dashing, daring, even foolhardy, overwhelmed by superior forces and, eventually, self destructive.

CHAPTER 10

A Clansman at Culloden

A Short Story by
Rennie McOwan

I WAS happy although exhausted that night I lay in the dark in the heather and the sharp prong of my targe and the handle of my dirk kept sticking into my side when I tried to snatch some sleep.

I wrapped myself more tightly in my Cameron war plaid and tried to doze until the order we had all been waiting for would be given to us. By that time you could have said that we were desperate men because there were thousands of us lying hidden in the heather, occasionally muttering as rain and sleet soaked the moor and the April wind which still had the taste of winter snow and ice about it worked its way through the hollows of the peat hags and set the birches and the alders quivering on a small mound where our chiefs sat in a small group quietly conversing.

All around were the big Highland hills still white with snow and as I shifted my sword to get a more comfortable sleeping position I wondered how many of us by nightfall the next day would still see the snow on the hills and smell the scent of wet birch and heather after rain.

Just before I drifted off to sleep I thought of these months that had passed, of how we had marched in ranks to join the Prince and the other Jacobite chiefs at Glenfinnan.

We were late in arriving and some of the men laughed to themselves that we had done that by design because by the time the Cameron contingents arrived at the mustering place the MacDonalds and Stewarts had gathered and our absence had been noticed and I think it could have truthfully been said that there would have been no rising if our chief, Lochiel, had not called us out.

Anyway, whether I was to be alive or dead tomorrow, I remembered it well, that great day when our piper crested the brae and we followed on behind him, our weapons shining, our plaids flapping in the breeze and we could see all the faces down below looking towards us and cheering broke out as we tramped downhill and everyone knew that the Rising was now a reality.

I've slept in a lot of odd places since then, lying among rushes at Gladsmuir just before our first battle when we swept General Cope's men from the field and in barns and sheds and behind walls when we made our long march into England only to find that the French had not landed, the English Jacobites did not rush to join us, and with London almost within our grasp, our leaders felt that we should return to the Highlands and there try and capture the hated Hanoverian force and then, joined by other clans, we would come again in the Spring.

I remember, too, falling asleep through exhaustion during the retreat from Clifton, in the north of England, when one of the Glengarry MacDonalds who had fought a disciplined rearguard action kicked me to my feet and made me march on when all I wanted to do was to fall down and sleep.

Most men find it hard to sleep before a battle and that was certainly true at Falkirk when the Hanoverian army caught up with us and even brought their own hangmen to execute those of us who would become prisoners of war, but we showed them.

We were not beaten yet and under our great military commander, General Lord George Murray, we sent them packing yet again and I can remember to this day seeing some of the MacDonald clansmen lying flat on the heather as the dragoons thundered towards them and then nimbly wriggling sideways to avoid the hooves as the horses galloped over them and then, with one blow, bringing down both horse and rider. It takes great courage and timing to do that and it was something I could never manage myself, but I think I did well enough when the charge was ordered and the blood sprang to the head and we rushed towards the enemy.

All this went through my mind as I tried to sleep because another battle was upon us and this time we were not in such good heart.

Many of the men were very tired and some had gone back to their own glens to see to the safety of their families because reports had come in that the Hanoverian soldiers and their Campbell allies had been burning the homesteads in some of the land owned by clans who had joined the Prince.

I am sorry to say that our leaders had begun to fall out with one another at this stage over what should be done next and we had sent sizeable contingents of the army, including the MacPhersons, into other areas.

That was necessary to deal with groups of the enemy but it weakened our main army. We were all accustomed to living off nothing more than oatmeal at this stage but even that was beginning to run out and many of the men were hungry.

We were not at our best to fight a pitched battle but as I had joined in one of our charges three times now and had seen us victorious each time I thought that we could still do it again.

But then came news of a different kind. General Cumberland, with a large army, was encamped not far from us and our chief and others decided we would attack his camp at night. The more we thought about it, the more we all felt the idea had our enthusiasm because we knew that our rush would take us past the sentries and in among the tents before Cumberland's men had time to grab their arms. We knew from our patrols that he was not certain where we were and would probably not expect such an attack.

All this passed through my mind as I tried to sleep, but I needn't have bothered because suddenly a figure in a feathered bonnet was bending over me and I was being told to pick up my weapons and to quietly follow the man in front of me until I got further orders.

I think I will remember that night forever.

By this time we were all hardened campaigners and, in the pale light of the moon which occasionally flickered through the dark clouds, I could see long lines of men creeping forward, their weapons hidden inside their plaid so that no gleam would catch a sentry's eye, their deer-hide footwear making no sound in the heather and their targes slung on their backs.

From all over the moor they came and I think we must have had at least a couple of thousand men and I learned later that some others had been held back as a reserve force.

Every now and then a whisper would come down the line and the man in front of me would turn round and say: "We've to halt until further orders. There's to be no talking and no movement" and I remember crouching anxiously there, the sweat chilling on me in the night wind, until another whisper came down the line and we were ordered to slip forward once more.

Ahead of us in the dark I could see the black outline of the crest of the moor and we were halted just below it and asked to spread out sideways in long lines, again with no talking and no noise and by this time we had one or two stragglers because, as I said, some of the men were very hungry. Then we were ordered forward to just below the crest.

We learned in detail later what had happened, how Lord George Murray had carefully checked out the enemy's camp and led us to the point where sentries were less numerous and the camp at its most vulnberable because below the crest lay a wide burn and then grassy flat ground and moorland on which were pitched hundreds of tents with the mouth of the camp, so to speak, at the far side around which had been built makeshift barriers on which fieldpieces had been mounted.

The Hanoverian army had used the high ground that we had crossed as a kind of wall behind them and they did not expect a Highland rush from that side.

I suppose all of the sentries near the crest were killed. All I know is that I saw the body of one of them just below the crest and could make out his red coat and crossbelts in the dim light and standing over him was one of our lads with a dirk in his hand.

Then our commanders hurried along the line, again whispering more orders. We were to charge over the crest, down the other side, across the burn, through the tents, thereby taking the gunners and the sentries at the other side in the rear. We were not to stop for our own wounded. We were not to stop for anything. Every figure coming out of a tent was to be treated as an enemy and cut down.

We were to be careful that in the dark we did not accidentally shoot or stab any of our own men and were instructed that once the charge reached the far side of the camp orders would be given for our men to halt, rally and charge back through the camp a second time. We were told that other parties had been sent further down the strath to cut off fugitives and to warn us of any unexpected reinforcements.

I remember it still, the pacing sentries in the gloom below, the stacks of arms, the white tents, the tethered horses, little pennons flying from some of the tents showing where officers slept and groups of soldiers sitting chatting round huge fires while others lay sleeping on the ground, their arms beside them.

I can't say I can remember too much about what happened next because it all passed so quickly and yet it must have been upwards of an hour.

By that time in the campaign we were fighting mad, and when the order to charge came we went over the crest and down the slope like stags coming down a hillside, roaring our heads off in our clan slogan: "O sons of dogs, come here and I will give you flesh."

On each side of us, Stewarts and MacDonalds and MacLachlans and others all did the same and although our army was organised by this time into proper regiments, nevertheless it was second nature for most of us to fight as a clan body.

We were across the stream in seconds and in among them. We slashed at the guy-ropes of tents bringing them down, we stabbed at the occupants through the canvas, all around there were screams and shouts and our pipers on the ridge behind played the old war tunes.

I remember men looming up in front of me and cutting them down like nettles and rushing on only to find others doing the same and once I had to take a blow from a musket butt on my targe and I was knocked to the ground by another soldier, but some of the MacDonalds running forward on my right dealt with them and I was able to get up again and run on and so it went on until we were in among the cannon and cutting down the gunners in a huge melee of shouting and cursing men.

It became increasingly difficult to spot friend from foe in the half-dark and shouts from our leaders and the sound of the pipes brought most of us together at the far side of the camp and we could partly see and hear little knots of the enemy running downstream and clambering out of the base of the strath and we left them to be dealt with by our patrols and by our reserve force.

By this time some of the Hanoverian soldiers had managed to load muskets or to fix bayonets and they were forming defensive groups and one volley from them into the darkness brought down some men near me, but again the orders to charge were given and we crashed back again through the tents and there was nothing for it, but to cut and slash and parry until some of our stragglers got up on the crest of the ridge with a piper and succeeded in making such a racket that the enemy thought another battle force had arrived and they began to surrender.

As the light improved we saw that we had won a crushing victory. A Highland broadsword wielded by experienced men can wreak dreadful havoc and the floor of the strath was littered with corpses and with wounded men. Lochiel gave orders that the prisoners were to be gathered together at one side and there were many of these. The only sad bit for us was that Cumberland and some of his staff had escaped and they may have been in one of the groups that we heard clattering down the glen.

As the early morning light came in we counted our booty and our losses. We did not have many killed but we did have a fair number of wounded, some, I am sorry to say, as a result of blows from their comrades in the half-dark and before identity could be established. The booty was very great and we captured much needed supplies, cheese, biscuits, flour and oatmeal, plus bottles of wine and other liquor which soon vanished.

We set out to spike the cannon so that they could not be used again and we broke all the muskets that we could and we piled all their ammunition that we did not need for ourselves into a huge heap and then, having marched all the men and horses back from it for about a mile, we lit a trail of gunpowder and up it went in an enormous roar that could have been heard in Inverness.

Ah, that was a great night. We had thrashed our enemy yet again and surely now, well-armed and provisioned once again, we had gained time.

Surely now the French would come and the other clans would rise and more and more men would see that our Prince, Tearlath, was the rightful possessor of the throne of Britain.

My tired mind tried to grasp all this and sleep came and went and all of a sudden I felt a great chill come over my body and a great weariness possessed my spirit. I started when a hand was placed on my shoulder and I saw a man's face in a feathered bonnet bend over mine in the early hours of the morning and say: "Wake up, lad. Wake up. They're here. They're here."

And I realised that I was not on a dark moor but lying sleeping in heather alongside the great grey walls of Ruthven Barracks in Badenoch which we had captured earlier in the campaign and all around me were men from several clans, thousands of them, still with their weapons but tired and weary-looking.

Close by I could see other Highlanders who looked like the MacPhersons and I was surprised because I knew that they had been campaigning elsewhere.

I was exhausted because a few days before I had taken part in that last desperate charge of the clans on Culloden Moor, when we were shot at and cut down by grapeshot and cannon fire for what seemed like hours before the men could stand it no longer and charged the Hanoverian ranks. It was a mistake and badly timed and hundreds fell dead but we smashed through their front line and might well have done the same to the second but we were outnumbered and exhausted and had to leave the field.

Our cause seemed lost and the remnants of our army were urged to make for Ruthven Barracks which was to be the new rallying point.

Despite that terrible day on Culloden Moor and the loss of so many dear friends I could see that we were still a force to be reckoned with because contingents of our army had been elsewhere under orders when Culloden was fought and had now returned. Tired though I was my spirits rose when I realised that we now had more men at Ruthven than we were able to muster at Culloden and the fight could go on.

Even over the years I cannot bear to tell without weeping what happened next.

Our leaders were no longer united, the Prince bade us return to our homes and look to our own safety and that of our families and he then left to go into hiding and eventual exile.

Many of the men wept and some shouted protests at him and some said they would fight on as guerillas.

As for me, I sat with my head on my knees, sick with the knowledge and the memory that the real night-attack on Cumberland's camp had been cancelled and what I had seen and felt had only been the kind of dream exhausted men have at times of tension and danger.

Many a time in future years, wielding a sword in other lands for other men's causes, I thought of that dream and its vivid memories.

It was a dream that could very easily have been reality and, if so, the story of the Highlands and of my country would have been very, very different.

Would that it had been so.

CHAPTER 11

On The Bonnie Prince Charlie Trail

A GOOD place to start off the Bonnie Prince Charlie tourist trail is the same place he began - the Western Isles.

At the Western Isles Tourist Board, 26 Cromwell Street, Stornoway, Isle of Lewis (tel. 0851 703088) the staff will give you all the details about the Prince's adventures in the Hebrides, both at the beginning of his Scottish adventure and at the end, and point out places of interest.

Further south the Tourist Information Centre at Portree, Skye, (tel. 0478 612137) is also a treasure trove of information.

The island also has the Clan Donald Library and Study Centre (tel. 0471 844389) which gives details of the local population's involvement in the Rebellion and the various punishments that were consequently meted out to them.

Crossing to the mainland, a 'must' visit is to the monument at Glenfinnan, 18 miles west of Fort William, where the clans first gathered in strength.

The monument was erected in 1815 by Alexander Macdonald of Glenaladale and has a Highland soldier on the top.

There is a visitors centre at which the main events of the whole campaign are recounted.

Although Fort George near Inverness was built two years after the Rebellion as a deterrent to potential future rebels, the museum there still has Jacobite memorabilia and is always well worth a visit if only to see the strength of the Government response to the '45.

Culloden Moor is a must for all visitors, of course.

Now run by the National Trust (tel.0463 790607), features of interest include the clan graves which are the communal burial places with simple headstones bearing individual clan names alongside the main road; the great memorial cairn erected in 1881; the Well of the Dead, a single stone

with the inscription 'The English were buried here'; Old Leanach farm-
house now restored to a battle museum; and the Cumberland Stone from
which the Duke of Cumberland is said to have viewed the scene.

The Visitors Centre has an exhibition, study room, restaurant, bookshop
and audio-visual programme in various languages. There is a big collection of weapons and portraits.

The Round Tower at Inverness Castle and the Duke of Cumberland's
Headquarters at Viewfield Stables in Nairn also have exhibitions. For further information about them tel. 01463 234353.

Travelling south, the next stop should be Ruthven Barracks, half a mile
from Kingussie.

Once the site of a fortress occupied by the Wolf of Badenoch, it was cre-
ated into Hanoverian barracks in 1734 by General Wade. It was here in
1746 after Culloden that the Highlanders held their last despairing rally
and despite being still a powerful force were given the message to look to
their own safety as the cause was lost. In despair they blew up the barracks
and the ruins can still be viewed and the atmosphere of gloom felt by the
more sensitive visitor.

The next stop is Blair Castle near Pitlochry where the Prince stayed when
his army passed through this spectacular stretch of Highland countryside.

The Jacobites besieged it prior to Culloden after it had fallen into
Hanoverian hands thus making it the last castle in Britain to have been
besieged. There is a fine collection of Jacobite relics, a restaurant, visitors
centre and nature trail.

Pressing on to Edinburgh, an obvious place to stop is Holyrood House
where the Prince held his brief court during the triumphal opening phase
of his campaign.

The National Library of Scotland on the George 1V bridge (tel.0131 226
4531) is also a rich source of Jacobite memorabilia as are the Museum of
Antiquities and the Scottish National Portrait Library at 1 Queen Street
(tel.0131 556 8921) and the Royal Museum of Scotland in Chambers
Street (tel.0131 225 7534).

Next stop is Callendar House, near Falkirk. The Prince enjoyed the hos-
pitality of the house when he passed through the area and there are also
details of the battle of Falkirk won by the Jacobites prior to their final
defeat. For further details on visiting times tel. 0324 612134.

Travelling on to Glasgow, the Tourist Board at 39 St. Vincent Place (tel.
0141 204 4400) have details of Jacobite connections. Glasgow Green can
still be walked over where the Prince reviewed his troops on their retreat

north and the house where he stayed at the corner of the Trongate and Glassford Street has a prominent plaque on the wall. The Art Gallery and Museum at Kelvingrove also has Jacobite relics.

Travelling south, the local tourist centre in Dumfries will supply details of Jacobite connections and the same is true across the border at Carlisle and Derby.

By car and with a detailed itinerary, a pleasant, leisurely fortnight's holiday can be spent on the Bonnie Prince Charlie trail touring much of northern Britain from the golden sands of the Western Isles to the rich farmlands of England.

For any further information the best source is the Central Information Unit, Scottish Tourist Board, 23 Ravelston Terrace, Edinburgh EH4 3EU (tel. 0131 332 2433; fax. 0131 332 9212.)

CHAPTER 12

The Rebel Clansman Portrayed

Here are some of the clans who supported the House of Stewart during the 1745 Rebellion.

ALL · MY · HOPE · IS · IN · GOD

Clan Fraser

The leaders of the Frasers were always devious when it came to supporting the Jacobite cause and always left their options open until the last moment.

Simon Fraser, the 11th Lord Lovat who was known as 'the Old Fox', tried to hedge his bets by sending out his son with the clansmen supporting the Prince.

His deviousness did him little good - he was beheaded as a rebel in 1747.

Clan Gordon

The Gordons from Aberdeen and Banff were strongly represented in the Jacobite ranks, including 400 infantry and numerous cavalry.
  Gordon of Glenbucket and Lord Lewis Gordon were the leaders.
  They were decimated by English grapeshot during the opening phase of Culloden.

Clan Macdonald

The Macdonalds of Keppach were descended from the Lords of the Isles and their history is one of constant warfare.

They joined the Rebellion at Glenfinnan and remained loyal to the end.

They were ferocious fighters, always to the front, and much feared by the Hanoverians.

CRAGAN·AN·FHITHICH

Clan MacDonell

The MacDonells of Glengarry had a raven in their crest, reflecting Norwegian descent.

They constantly supported the Jacobite cause and fought with Montrose. They were also at Killiecrankie and Sheriffmuir.

The whole clan was committed to the '45 Rebellion and suffered the consequences, losing their lives and their lands, the survivors being dispersed abroad.

Clan MacBain

The MacBains formed part of the Clan Chattan federation which joined the '45.
   They originated in the Lochaber district before being driven further east.
   Their history always was a martial one and Gillies MacBean was said to have been the bravest
and most ferocious fighter at Culloden.

Clan MacLachlan

The MacLachlans originated in Argyll before being dispossessed by the Campbells who remained loyal to the Crown.

They moved to Strathlachlan where they have remained strongly represented to this day.

They have a long, glorious history of martial prowess and some of their bravest men died at Culloden.

TOUT · PREST

Clan Murray

The Murrays were strongly represented in the Jacobite ranks, the outstanding member being Lord George Murray who became the army's general.

He managed to flee abroad to lifelong exile after Culloden but many of his clansmen died on the moor.

Others were rounded up and killed in the massacres following the quelling of the Rebellion.

Clan Ranald

The warlike branch of the Clan Ranald of Garmoran was descended from Ranald, son of John, first Lord of the Isles.

They were natural supporters of the House of Stewart and were adept at fighting, although this usually involved feuds with neighbouring clans.

They were a potent addition to the rebel ranks.

Rebellion

Clan Stewart

The Stewarts were, of course, foremost in supporting the Prince, particularly the Appin Stewarts who took part in all the major confrontations.

They were foremost among the clansmen who lamented when the decision was taken to retreat from Derby.

They gambled all on their cause - and lost all.

Clan Cameron

The Camerons were some of the first supporters of the Prince and seven hundred of them came marching down Glenfinnan, pipes skirling, when the Jacobite flag was unfurled.

Donald Cameron, "the gentle Lochiel", was instrumental, through his example, of giving the clans confidence at the outset of the Rebellion.

Clan MacGregor

The MacGregors had a long, turbulent history, constantly feuding with the neighbouring Campbells and fighting redcoats.

They took to the Rebellion like fish to water.

Being outlaws anyway they felt they had nothing to lose by pledging themselves to the House of Stewart.